Struggles, Trials, and Freedom

By

Mike Warren

Copyright © 2024 by - Mike Warren - All Rights Reserved.

It is not legal to reproduce, duplicate, or transmit any part of this document in either electronic means or printed format. Recording of this publication is strictly prohibited.

Dedication

This book is dedicated to God the Father, Jesus, and the Holy Spirit, for whom I would not be here today if not by the grace and mercy that has been abundantly been shown to me throughout all of my life. The loving kindness that has been given to me through not only the cross that Jesus bore for my sin, but that of which gives me peace, joy, and happiness, on a daily basis that allows me to face every situation that I encounter that surpasses all understanding and reasoning of the human mind. His unfailing love is what I desire and seek every morning that I wake and open my eyes up to a brand new beginning. The bible says that his mercies are renewed daily, and for that I am grateful far beyond any words that I could ever put to pen and paper. Even though he already knows how much I love him, I pray that this book will be a small gift to Him in appreciation for what He has done for me.

Many times throughout the writing of this book I sat and wept at how much I appreciate how he has loved me enough to call me not only his son, but that he calls me His friend as well. I pray that as you read this book, not only will you be able to find His strength for your life that will help carry you on to the next victory that he has for you, but that you will be able to feel just how much God loves you today.

I thank you Father for loving me enough to have a plan for my life, and sending your Son to die for me so that I might be reconciled back to you, in order to fulfill this plan. I thank you Jesus for being obedient all the way to the cross, so that I might be able to look past the agony of this world, and fix my eyes upon you and what you've done for me. I thank you Holy Spirit for not only being the comforter who allows me to feel Gods love, even when everything in this world would try and discourage me from fulfilling the will of God in my life, but that you live in me, and walk beside me as a friend.

"For God so loved the world that He gave His one and only Son, that whoever believes in Him shall not perish but have eternal life."

John 3:16

Table of Contents

Foreword 1
Chapter I 4
Chapter II 19
Chapter III 39
Chapter IV 49
Chapter V 56
Chapter VI 61
Chapter VII 68
Chapter VIII 75
Chapter IX 93
Chapter X 103
Chapter XI 108
Chapter XII 114

Foreword

Believing that God will work all of our trials and tribulations out for our benefit is a hard teaching to understand, especially when we are in the midst of the battles that we face in life. It is so easy to feel like we are in this all alone, and no one understands what we are going through when we are struggling with the situations that come upon us. The battle is in the mind, and not only does the enemy attack our bodies through pain and affliction, but he likes to attack our thoughts to try and make us feel like there is no good answer for the pain and suffering that we so often must endure. He likes to isolate us, cut us from the herd, and make us feel like there will be no end in sight to the problems that we are facing. It's very easy to slip into the mindset of believing that not only we have done nothing wrong to deserve what we are going through, but that if there is a loving God out there, how could he allow us to go through such hardships and tragedies in life.

Even after getting saved and coming into the knowledge of God when I was 20, I still had a hard time understanding why there needs to be so many disappointments that we will face throughout our lives. Even though I kept coming back to the fact that Adam and Eve allowed sin to come into this world, thus making it imperfect, I still wrestled with the reason why God continues to allow so many bad things to happen to people.

I finally began to except the fact that not only is sin still prevalent in this world, causing us to be deceived by taking our eyes off of God and focusing on our problems, but that God will use these situations to mold us into the image of himself that he so desires us to be. The bible tells us to be thankful in all of the circumstances that we will face in life, not just the good ones, but the ones that we consider to be too hard and unfair as well. His peace is there to help guide and comfort us through the circumstances that cause us to cry out in agony and question what good things could come from these situations. As believers in Christ, seeing the light at the end of the tunnel is easier to accomplish when we realize that the light is already inside of us, calling us to allow His spirit to guide us through every situation that we encounter along the way. Even the apostle Paul admits that he hasn't mastered these truths about God, but that he puts his faith and trust in Him anyway, moves forward, and doesn't look back.

As you read my story, I pray that if there is anything that you identify with about my life that you haven't allowed God to heal you from, you will find that healing and peace that surpass all understanding that is waiting for you on the other side.

Chapter I

I grew up in a typical middle-class home in central Oregon, where I was the middle child with a brother who was 3 older and a baby brother who was 7 years younger than me. We lived out in the woods about 20 minutes south of Bend, Oregon, at the base of the Cascade mountain range that had enough room for two boys, as my baby brother was too young, to spend all of their time outside not driving my mom crazy. Some of my fondest memories are filled with climbing trees, going down to the creek, and playing hide and go seek until we were called back to the house by either my mother or my father calling out in a voice that would travel across acres of wilderness, with seemingly endless echoes of our names reverberating off of the vast amounts of trees and hills we were surrounded by.

"Jimmy, Michael, time to come home."

We would respond, "Coming."

And then we would run back home as fast as we could, jumping over fallen trees and sidestepping broken stumps, making sure not to accidentally step into any one of the numerous red carpenter ant piles that could easily be mistaken for just large piles of pine needles that would blend in with the forest floor. After learning that we could start fires with our magnifying glasses, we would try and see how many ants we could burn up before being chased away by the pungent smell of their formic acid they would deploy as a defense mechanism. Sometimes, I would take my glasses off and see how much of the annoying liquid I could collect on them before I would have to retreat rubbing my eyes and nose.

We learned how far we could wander off and still hear their voices by trial and error. Travel too far, and at the very least we would be met with unhappy parents when we returned. If we were too late in returning, we probably wouldn't get to leave the confines of our 1-acre property the next day. Even though we had plenty enough room to run around on our own property, it just wasn't the same when we weren't allowed to venture off into the great unknown like our heroes, Daniel Boone and Davy Crockett.

The Deschutes River was only a little over a mile from our house, and we would go fishing down there as much as we could talk at least one of our parents into taking us there. We weren't allowed to go to the river on our own, as they thought it was too dangerous for us to venture off by ourselves. The river was almost too cold to swim in as it doesn't have much time to warm up due to the fact that it is created from snow melt coming directly off of the Cascade Mountains and was full of undercurrents that would pull you down and more than likely keep you there. They also used to take us down there in the winter time when the river would overflow into the marsh area and freeze up, making for a great ice skating area. Mom would make hot cocoa and sandwiches for everyone as Jim and I were piling on the warm cloths and rounding up our ice skates for the highlight of our week. When we would get there, the first thing dad would do as we were putting on our skates was to make a nice warm fire for us to come back to when it was time to get some coco and refuel. We would spend a few hours chasing each other around the iced-over field until our parents got tired of being there and decided that it was time to go back home and call it a day. As kids, we would never be done thinking we had spent enough time gliding around on the ice and would count the days until we could return.

I used to love to climb trees, so living out in a forest suited me just fine. One day, when I was about 5, I set out to climb as high up as I could in this pine tree just outside the back door. I was just hanging out up there, probably about 50-60 feet off the ground, when my mom came outside to call me in for lunch. I was by myself that day as I wasn't old enough for 1st grade, and my brother was in school. I didn't attend kindergarten because I wasn't ready to leave the comfort of my mother yet, and she home-schooled me, so I had a lot of playtime. She yelled,

"Michael, time to come in the house for lunch."

I yelled back, "OK, be right down."

She was puzzled at the fact she couldn't tell where my voice was coming from and yelled again,

"Where are you at?"

I yelled back, "Up here!"

She asked, "Where up here?"

I responded, "Up here in the tree."

As she looked up and up the tree until she finally saw me, she did her best not to sound frantic and scare me into falling, as she hadn't seen me that far up in a tree yet. To that point, I had only been maybe 10' up in one. She yelled back in as calm of a voice as she could,

"OK, it's time for lunch. Take your time."

Then, she went back into the house without watching the towering tree descend as fast as I could. She didn't want to watch me just in case I fell. When dad got home from work, she made him take his chainsaw and cut off all the branches he could reach so as to keep me from climbing it again. I remember thinking that this was, at best, a futile attempt to save me as we lived in the middle of the forest that had trees spaced out about every 15 feet away from each other. But when a woman wants to feel safe or protect her children, she doesn't always use reasoning the way a man does.

One time, when I was around 6, we were outside doing boy things out by the main dirt road that was lined with smaller trees so as to give us privacy from passing cars with one of the older neighbor kids, I ended up climbing a small pine tree just to pass the time. Most of those trees were only, on average, from seedling size up to around 15 feet tall. As I reached the point of climbing one of the larger ones, just before the tree would bend and fall over, one of the neighbor boys decided that he would follow me up the tree as well. Due to the fact that he was older and bigger than both my brother, I looked down and told him that the tree was too small for both of us to be in at the same time. Well, he wasn't going to listen to this little kid and proceeded to climb up the small tree even further. I knew that the tiny little tree couldn't handle the weight of both of us at the same time, so I started to make my way back down and tree to alleviate some of the stress on my top half of the tree. But before I could climb far enough down, the tree started bending over with me ending upside down and falling smack-dab on top of one of those hard limbs that are growing up instead of out and are half dead with a knot and a pointed spike on the tip of it. When I hit the ground, and started to realize the gravity of what had just happened. I remember seeing stars and knowing I was going to need my mom, who was in the house at the time, to take away my pain and make me feel better.

As I started crying and making my way back across our red-cindered driveway, I was greeted by my mother, who wiped away some of the blood off of my head and began giving me kisses to help calm me down.

Well, when I saw the blood on her hand, it just made me cry even harder as I struggled to catch my breath and breathe without convulsing the way a child does when they get really upset. I had worked myself up into quite the crying frenzy as I wiped away tears and snot from my face. She took me into the house and laid me down on a blanket in front of an electric organ that my parents used to play, and started playing and singing one of the many songs she knew in order to help calm me down. I remember thinking to myself, why was she playing that stupid organ instead of attending to her youngest child, me. I was still the youngest at the time because Jason wasn't in the picture yet, as he wouldn't be born for about another and a year and a half or so; so why wasn't she giving me all of her attention right now? I remember being able to muster up some words and cry out to the universe,

"Why does everything always happen to me? Why am I the one that always has to get hurt?"

My mom just looked down and smiled at me as she continued to play that darned electric organ until I had settled down and stopped crying.

It is true though. I was always hurting myself in some form or fashion that would require my mom to patch me up and take away the pain only the way that a mother can. There's just something about a mother's love that can't be replaced by anyone else on earth. Even a loving father just doesn't seem to carry the same measure of empathy as that of a mother. The fact that they carry us around inside of their bodies for over 9 months before we enter into this world really does make the difference. They just seem to instinctively know what we need to make the world a better place for us and comfort us in away like no other. Hugs and kisses from a mother are like medicine to the soul as they take away all the bad feelings and minor pain we encounter in life, whereas fathers usually just try and minimize the situation by telling you to rub some dirt on it and stop crying. Both tactics have their place in a child's life as we're growing up, neither one being better than the other. This is the importance of having both parents being around at the same time when raising a child; we need both the soothing comfort of a mother's love when times are down and the strong presence of a father to help us understand that life is probably not as bad as we think it is.

I remember feeling like I could conquer anything in life that came my way when we lived out in the woods. My brother and I were true adventurers who had no limits to our abilities or imaginations. One time, when I was about 8, we were so confident that when mom got mad at us for something we shouldn't have been doing, we responded by telling her that we were going to run away and go live on our own out in the woods. I remember this creepy yet happy smile on her face that was a little scary as she thought about what we had just said.

She responded by saying, "Ok. Make sure you boys take some extra cloths for when it gets cold."

We thought no problem. We just went into our bedroom that we shared in our two-room trailer house, put on some extra clothes, and then returned to the kitchen to get some food for the new life we were about to embark on, just to have our mother say,

"Oh no, you're not getting any of my food. You guys are going to have to find your own food. And just know that when you walk outside that door, you can't come back."

After thinking about the struggles that our new journey would pose and having a small conversation, we decided that it would probably be in our best interest if we stayed at home and put up with the unbearable life that we were subjected to. Her response was just,

"Ok, that's fine too. But you will apologize and never speak to me like that again. And you can go spend the rest of the day in your bedroom."

Life was starting to get a little complicated at that point. It seemed like the choices I was starting to face were not as easy as I had expected them to be. It was time to start learning the hard lessons.

My dad decided to turn our property into a little farm and started buying animals. He bought us a Shetland pony we named Daisy, and after making a little circular arena out of some of the trees on the property for her, he brought her home. My grandpa Warren bought a new saddle for us and brought it out for us to ride her for the first time. After getting her ready to ride, my grandpa asked,

"Who's gonna to be the first to ride her?"

Without hesitation, I responded,

"I will."

Even though my dad wanted my older brother to ride her first, Jim had no objections to allowing his little brother to test the waters first. I was excited and full of courage to ride this new pony we had received. As my grandpa helped me mount her, I was filled with so much pride and joy that it allowed me to confidently take the reins and ride that pony. We knew she had been one of those ponies that had been retired from the carnival where she was attached to one of those mechanisms with other ponies that would allow children to ride around in a circle, and parents wouldn't have to worry about their children being carried away, but what we didn't know was that she was retired early because she was mean. As I took the reins and started off, all of a sudden, she started running and trying to buck me off. When we rounded the first turn, as I tried to stay on, she was successful in throwing me off directly over the top of her head as I landed squarely on my backside. At 7 years old, I started crying and didn't want to have anything more to do with her. When I got up, I started dusting myself off and headed for the fence to end this little adventure. I heard my grandpa say,

"Oh no. You're gonna get back up on that horse and show her who the boss is."

I responded by saying, "I don't wanna show her who the boss is. I wanna go inside now."

Grandpa says, "Nope, You're gonna get back up on that horse and ride her."

I looked at my dad for some saving grace but got none. He, too, told me that I had to get back on her and finish what I had started. I turned and looked at my brother Jim just to see a big smirk on his face shaking his head in agreement with them. Up until this point, I had never wanted to do something less in my short little life than what I was facing at that moment. Reluctantly, I got back up on Daisy and finished my ride without a hitch in my giddy-up this time.

What's funny is that I would end up being the only one she would allow to ride her. She would either turn around, bite you on your leg, or she would commence bucking you off, or both. She ended up bucking my older brother off and sent him flying into the fence. He didn't have a shirt on, and the wooden fence my dad had built didn't have the bark stripped off, so he got scraped up pretty good. He never did ride her again, so it was just me and Daisy. I would go out to the arena, saddle her up, and ride her for hours. I would find it so relaxing that if I wasn't paying attention, I would fall asleep, and she would head over to her shelter that was just taller than her, and the top post would hit me in the chest and knock me off. But I didn't care. I would get up, climb back up on her, and ride some more.

My dad decided to try his hand at raising pigs, also. Well, I should say try our hands, as we were the ones that had to feed them. I remember the smell of the slop that he bought for them that came in bags that we had to add water to and thinking it smelt pretty good, almost like oatmeal. They weren't too much work until they got out, and we had to chase them around the woods yelling,

"Here, little piggy piggy, come on back, little piggy piggy. We need to eat you."

My mom was elated when it came time to round them up and send them off to the slaughter. She hated their very existence and wanted them gone from the day dad brought them home. She didn't like the sound or the smell of them. She was happy just to have some rabbits, a dog, and some outside cats that kept the mice at bay. Along with two boys and a baby, she felt she had enough on her plate.

By the end of my second-grade year, they had sold the farm, and we moved into Bend; mom had begun to decide that she could not stay married to dad anymore. I had started to notice that they were arguing with each other to the point where Mom was always crying about something and didn't appear to be happy anymore. I never knew what the source of their arguments was about; I just knew that she wasn't happy being married to him anymore. Dad had received an inheritance that allowed him to purchase a restaurant that he would run and a flower shop for mom to explore her more creative side. But not even their new business endeavors would be enough to keep them together. So, after less than two years, Mom filed for divorce, and the family was broken up.

It was decided that my older brother Jim would stay with dad, and my baby brother Jason and I would move out and on with mom. Going to three different schools during my 4th-grade year was definitely eye-opening. The confidence and security that I once had seemed to be slipping away from me as I encountered a brand-new world filled with uncertainty and ambiguity. I had to start trying to fit in at the new schools I was attending by making new friends every time we moved. This is where I begin to find out that not everyone wants to be friends with the new kid. Not only did they not want to be friends, they wanted to pick on me.

Chapter II

Dealing with bullies would become a part of my everyday life, and I began to chip away at my personality and perspective on life as I once knew it. The old saying, "sticks and stones may break my bones, but names will never hurt me," is not true. Not only did I have to start defending myself physically by getting into fights, I had to start figuring out how to defend my feelings. The latter is way harder than the former. The words that would come out of the mouths of other children were so much harder to deal with than getting into any physical altercation. Not only did I not have a dad at home, I wore glasses and didn't have the right cloths on.

Dealing with these issues was hard enough as they were; having other children point them out to me on a daily basis became excruciating and unbearable at times.

I would return home from school to whichever apartment we lived in at the time, sometimes after running from older bullies, and spend the rest of my day crying and yearning for the life I had once had back in the comfort of the woods. I could smell the pine trees and hear the rushing water of the creek as I was having a hard time processing the changes that life was throwing at me at an accelerated rate. I couldn't find many things to be happy about and used to ask God, "why me?" Why did I have to go through this embarrassment and degradation of life as the other kids had everything I once had?

One of the many times I went to bed hungry, I remember asking God if he would please send me a sandwich. I told him that I promised not to tell anyone he gave it to me if he would just make it appear somewhere on my bed or anywhere in my room, for that matter. I didn't care where he put it; I was just so hungry that food and God were all that I could think about. Of course, no sandwich came, and my faith in God began to wane even further as I cried myself to sleep, wondering when this wretched way of life would finally end for me.

One time, after mom had sold her flower shop and moved us to Medford, OR, my third school, my 4th-grade year, I was walking home from school, and this older kid started running towards me and yelling that he was going to beat me up. I had no idea what set him off, and I had no intention of sticking around to find out why. I started running, but I could see he was going to catch up to me, so I stopped at a house that had the front door open and yelled for help. The man inside came to the door, and as I explained my situation to him, he told me that he wouldn't help and that I needed to leave. Fortunately, when I turned around, the bully had started walking back in the direction that he had come from, the opposite way I was heading. He continued to chase me home for about a week until, one day, I decided to stop. I'd had enough of running and decided I was going to make a stand and let chips fall where they may. My fear had turned to anger. I felt like I could take on anyone at this point. As I turned around to confront this kid, he stopped in his tracks, turned around and went back in the direction he had come from. I remember thinking, wow, is that all you have to do to get a bully to leave you alone? The next day in school, I saw him outside the front of the school and walked up to him. I asked him why he had been chasing me all this time just to have him say,

"You didn't hold the door open for me when you walked into the school one day, and I got locked out."

I had no idea what he was talking about, and I told him so. We ended up being friends for the rest of the time I stayed there in Medford, which was only until the school year had finished, and I moved back to my dad's. That was my first lesson in life that taught me that standing up to bullies and confronting the fears in life that can and will keep you running need to be dealt with. I learned that you can't just simply run away from your problems in life; they need to be confronted and dealt with before you can have any peace and properly move on with your life.

Even though I started standing up for other people by the time I was in the 3rd grade, before my parents had divorced, I suppose these experiences that I had are the reason why I so easily took on the role of being a protector and standing up for the weak became second nature to me.

The first time I stood up to a bully for someone else was when a kid in the 4th grade started picking on a friend of mine while we were on lunch recess at school. My friend found me on the playground and told me this other kid in the 4th grade was threatening to beat him up for no reason. He pointed the boy out to me across the playground, and we marched over to confront him about the situation. As we got closer, I began to notice that not only was this kid a year older than us, but he looked like he could have been three years older. But I wasn't going to back down and let him continue to bully my friend, so when we approached him, I asked him why he was picking on my friend. With a smirk on his face, he simply replied,

"Because I can, what are gonna to do about?"

I said, "I'm gonna to make you stop."

He replied, "How are gonna to do that?

I came back with a,

"I'll fight you if that's what it's gonna take."

He said, "That's exactly what it's gonna take."

I accepted his challenge, and we agreed to meet up on the turf after school, as neither one of us wanted to get suspended for fighting.

After coming to the realization of how big this kid was, I found my older brother, who was in the 6th grade and asked him to help us out. I told him the situation, and his response was,

"Is he picking on you?"

I said "No. But he's picking on my friend."

Much to my disappointment, he said,

"If he's not picking on you, you'll have to handle yourself. Figure it out on your own."

Well, I decided that I couldn't back out now, and so we ended up meeting after school on the turf as planned. Along with my brother and around 15 other kids circling us, we decided it was time to fight. The bully asked me once again if this was something that I really wanted to do. I assured him that most definitely was, and we squared off as I put my fists up and acted like a boxer. Without landing any punches, I took a couple of jabs at him and moved around effortlessly, and I was more nimble than he was. He started closing in on me, so I took a couple of steps backwards just to have some unknown kid push me in the back, sending me stumbling forward towards my opponent. Just when I looked up to catch my balance, I was met with a right cross that caught me in the left eye, sending me backwards and landing on the ground. I had just gotten knocked out by this behemoth of a kid who showed no mercy whatsoever.

When I finally woke up, my older brother was standing over me, shaking my body, trying to wake me up. I got up off the ground and asked,

"Where'd everyone go?"

Jim said, "They all left, the fight's over."

After still being a little woozy from just being knocked out, I asked,

"Did I win?"

Jim assured me that I did not win. But he told me that while I was lying on the ground having nice dreams, he confronted the other kid about being a bully, to which the kid apologized for what he'd done. To my disappointment, we both walked home and called it a day.

The next day at school, sporting my new shiner, the bully found me on the playground and apologized for what he had done. He also apologized to my friend, who was standing next to me, and said he wasn't going to act like that anymore. He told me that he really respected me for standing up for my friend even though he knew that I figured that I was going to get my butt kicked in the process. We didn't end up being friends, but every time we saw each other after that, we would say hello and ask each other what was going on.

One time in the 5th grade, while living with my mom, who had moved to Astoria OR after leaving Medford, I ran into another bully who liked to try and embarrass me in front of the other kids. He used the same tactics as the other kids I had already run into at the previous schools I had attended. Making fun of my glasses, my clothes, and the rundown apartment complex that we lived in, he would push the limits of my kindness. When I would stand up for myself on the playground, he would only test me as far as he could without starting a fight, then walk away, leaving the other kids laughing at me. After school one day, while we were waiting out in front for our perspective buses to show up, he started in on me again. Now that school was out, and I wasn't concerned about the teachers getting involved, I challenged him to a fight.

I said, "You act really tough in front of all these other kids. Why don't you follow me down this path right here, and you and I can go fight without any other kids around? You think you're really tough in front of everyone else; let's see how tough you are when you're all alone?"

He looked at me with a surprised look on his face and said,

"No, I have to wait for my bus."

I said, "What, are you chicken?"

All of the other kids standing around said,

"Yeah, you're chicken?"

He responded, "No, I just have to wait for my bus. I don't want to miss it."

I told him, "I think you're chicken. And I don't want you to talk to me anymore after this. Keep your mouth shut, or I'm gonna pound on you."

His bus arrived first, and he got on and left the school with his head hung low. Everyone that was still there told me they thought he was chicken also and told me that what I had said to him was pretty cool. The next day in school, he started walking up to me while we were on the playground, and I took a defensive stance, anticipating a fight. He started shaking his head no and said,

"Hey, I don't want to fight you. I just wanted to apologize for the way I've been acting."

I unclenched my fists and told him,

"Ok. I accept your apology."

Then he said, "I have a motorcycle if you want to come over to my house this weekend and ride it. I already asked my parents, and they said that it was ok."

I told him no and said that I would be busy. But that it was cool of him to invite me. I never did take him up on his offer, as I didn't see where we could be friends after the way he treated me. We were cordial to each other for the rest of the school year, but never did end up being friends. That wasn't the bully I would ever come across, either.

One time, when I was in the 8th grade, my friends and I rode our bicycles over to a makeshift BMX track in a vacant dirt lot in Bend to do some daredevil jumping. We were being your typical 14-year-old boys trying to impress each other by seeing who could jump their bike the furthest without wiping out. The only ways you can accomplish this is by either going too fast and ending up flying over your handlebars as you came down on the front tire or by landing awkward on the frame of the bike when you finally came down out of the sky and hit the ground. If you were lucky, you didn't land on the parts that separate the boys from the girls and spend the next 10 minutes rolling around in the dirt, holding on to yourself, quietly calling on the name of your mother.

As we were all watching each other fearlessly launch our bodies through the air and secretly hoping to see the other guy wipeout worse than you had, I heard this younger boy who was around 8 or 9 years old running and yelling for help over a hill that separated the track from a rock field on the other side. When he got to our crowd of 5, he ran over to me and stood behind me, asking if I would protect him. I asked him what was going on, and he told me that he and a couple of other kids were playing in a rock fort, and some older kids chased them out of it. He told me that the other kids were saying they were going to beat them up, so they all scattered. Just then, I looked up to the top of the hill. He'd just come over and see a kid from my school who I knew was my age. When the bully saw the little kid was with us, he turned around and made his way back to his friends. Well, I didn't think it was good enough that they let the boys go. So, as I marched over the hill with my friends behind me, I found the other group of about 5 boys and asked them what was going on. They gave me the same story that the little boy had just told me and started laughing.

I said, "Well, I'm not a little boy. Why don't you come out of your fort and try to chase me off?"

Of course, it was the biggest kid in their group that stood up and accepted my challenge. He was a little bigger than I was, even though I was already around 5'10" and 130 pounds, but at this point, I didn't care; I was going to teach this kid a lesson about what happens to bullies.

I was so mad about the situation. I was going to fight him right in the middle of that rock field, but everyone there suggested that we move out into the open dirt area so it could be a better fight; either way, I didn't care. So we walked out to level ground and squared each other up. We both put our fists up in true boxing fashion and began to move around, waiting for the right moment to strike. I always put my fists up right in front of my face so I can block any would be punch thrown my way. I noticed that this kid only put his hands up to just below his chin, thus leaving his face exposed to any attack. I snickered to myself, knowing that I was pretty fast with a punch, and knew I was going to bloody this kid's face up good for him.

As I threw the first punch and hit him with a right cross on the left side of his face just below his eye, I watched him stagger back and catch his balance. I could tell by the look in his eyes that he was surprised at how fast I was and knew he was going to have his work cut out for himself today. I moved in for another one and blasted him with a left hook that rocked him backwards as he again had to catch himself from falling down. As I moved in for another right cross, he shot in towards my body, grabbing me around my waist and taking me to the ground. He was involved in wrestling at the school, so I knew he had some skills that I didn't possess that were going to make this lesson a little challenging. He managed to get on top of me with my back to the ground, but before he could hit me,

I grabbed on to both of his hands and rolled him off. I quickly jumped back up to my feet and moved back in for some more timely punches to his head as he was recovering, not giving him a chance to think about it. After hitting me a couple of more times in the face, he shot in again, grabbing me around my waist and trying to take me down one more time. I ended up spinning around and reaching down between my legs, as he now had me from behind, and grabbed his ankles. I pulled his legs towards me as hard as I could and threw my body back into his chest, causing us to fly backwards into the dirt. I immediately jumped to my feet, regaining my boxing stance, and moved in for some more punishment. But before I could get to him, he got up, turned away from me and started running in the opposite direction.

Well, I wasn't satisfied that his lesson in bullying was over, so I started chasing him just to have everyone say that he was hurt and didn't want to fight anymore. They told me that when we hit the ground, he landed on the corner of a cement slab that was behind us and couldn't fight anymore. At that point, I decided that the lesson was complete, and he could run home to mommy. I looked around for the little boy who was at the center of all this attention, but they told me he had long since run away and was nowhere to be found. I just wanted to make sure he got out of there ok, and they all told me he did.

After returning to school the next week, the word had gotten around that I had beaten up the biggest bully in the school. Other kids started coming up to me and congratulating me on my victory and telling me that the respected me for what I had done. I must admit it made me feel pretty darn good sticking up for little boy that day. That wasn't the first I'd had the opportunity to save someone else from the anguish that I had gone through as a younger boy, that one was definitely the sweetest victory that I'd had up to that point. I suppose that bully bore the brunt of all the times that I was pushed around growing up as an underdog, and it made me feel great.

A few more times during that school year, I would have other kids who were being bullied approach me and ask me if I could help them out. They would tell me that they had heard that I hated bullies and would probably help them with their problems as well. Some even offered me money if I would take on the challenge for them, which I never accepted. I loved standing up for the weaker kids and cherished the thought of being given another opportunity to put a bully in his place. I didn't even have to fight them anymore. I would just show up with the kid who was being bullied, and the bully would see me and ask if the kid was with me. I would respond by telling them that not only was the little kid with me but that if I heard that they continued to harass them, I would pound the crap out of them. I made this one bully walk his victim home every day and make sure no one else bothered him. He was like,

"Oh, come on, Warren, I don't have the time to do that."

I said, "If you have the time to bully him, you have the time to make sure he gets home safe. And he's going to tell me if you don't."

I don't know how long he walked that other kid home, but I never heard anything more about that one.

One more bully story, and I'll leave that subject alone.

When I was 16, we were kicking back partying at my older brother's duplex with his girlfriend when another friend showed up with a bloody lip and told us that he'd just gotten punched by a guy at a party he was at for burning out with his 1970 Firebird that had sent rocks flying into another guys car. It wasn't even the guy's car that punched him; I started to get cocky and asked him who punched him. When he revealed the name of the bully, I recognized him as the kid that I had beaten up back when I was in the 8th grade for picking on that little kid whom he had caught playing in his and his friend's fort. My friend who had just gotten decked for burning out was the same friend that I had stood up for back in the 3rd grade. We had been friends since the 1st grade, and I knew that he wasn't a fighter. I asked him how many guys were at the other party, and he said there were probably 10-15 guys hanging out. So my brother got on the phone and rounded up about another 6 guys to match the 6 guys that were already with us, and we made our way out to the Deschutes River Woods neighborhood to confront this guy. When we pulled up in the four vehicles that we had taken out there, the first guy out of the house to greet us was the said bully. I got out of my friend's Firebird and met the bully at the front of the car and asked him if he had punched my friend. He confessed that he had and apologized for going off on him. I said it wrong what he had done and wanted to shake my friend's hand that was still setting in his car. As I turned to motion for my friend to get out and come over to us, out of the corner of my right eye, I saw my older brother come running around me, saying,

"There's been enough talkn', it's time to punch somebody."

As he went to punch the guy, Jim slipped on something on the ground that he didn't see, because it was around 10:00 at night and dark out. Jim ended up falling into the guy, and the two of them stumbled around until they eventually gained their balance, and the fight was on. The bully was bigger than both Jim and I, so he had the advantage of both size and strength, and he knew how to use it. He ended up pushing Jim into the front left-hand quarter panel of one of our friend's trucks that had come out with us as a backup. As they were each trying to gain the upper hand on the other, I ran over and started punching the bully in the back of his head as hard and as fast as I could. Unfortunately for Jim, after about 4 or 5 punches, the bully moved his head to the right, and I nailed Jim right between the eyes with an overhand right. Jim yells out,

"Mike, that's me, bro."

Because I punched him between eyes, it took away some of his strength, which allowed the bully to take Jim down to the ground and get on top of him. With the bully on top of my brother's back now, he had the advantage to do what he wanted. But before he could get a punch off, I ran up and kicked the bully in the face like an NFL kicker on the opening kickoff drive of Super Bowl Sunday. He just sat there on top of Jim, trying to regain his senses, when I stepped back and let loose another championship kick to his chin. This time, the bully fell face-first into Jim's back and went limp. As Jim pushed the bully off of himself, the guy started moaning uncontrollably and just lay there motionless on the ground.

One of the other guys at the party yelled out he was going back into the house to get his rifle. Deciding it was time to leave, we all piled back into our vehicles and left because none of us had brought a gun with us.

As we made our way out of the housing area that encompassed several square miles and back out onto highway 97, we passed an ambulance with its lights and siren on heading back in the direction that we had just left.

We headed back to my brother's place, taking the back roads just in case the cops had been called, and continued to party. Reliving the moments that had just transpired, everyone was saying things like,

"Man, Mike, you don't have any mercy. I hope you're around if I ever get in a fight."

I really didn't feel any sense of adoration or take what was being said as a compliment. I just felt like I was in the moment, just doing what I had to do in order to take control of a situation. I wasn't going to let someone bully my friend, and I definitely wasn't going to let someone get over on my brother. I've always felt that family and friends were the most important things worth fighting for.

Chapter III

I spent the rest of my childhood moving back and forth between my mother and father as I needed to be with both of them and feel the love for both of them. Switching schools 12 times was definitely hard on me, but I needed to feel the presence and love of both parents as much as I could. Even if I couldn't have them both at the same time, moving back and forth between each parent gave me a temporary respite from the pain that the separation of my family had created. Neither one would say no when I would tell them I wanted to move back with the other parent. I would just pack up my belongings, we would meet up at a prescribed location in a different city, and I would feel a little better about my situation.

But within a month or two, the joy of being with one parent would be outweighed by the emptiness of not being with the other; I would continue to miss the days of having my family being together as one.

I used to like to spend time hanging around my Grandpa Warren whenever I had the chance; he always seemed to have an encouraging word and an abundance of knowledge to give his grandchildren. If we weren't just kicking back, watching him build a rifle or making a knife, we'd watch cartoons with him. He thought the Looney Tunes were the best. We'd be watching the Wile E. Coyote and the Road Runner, and he would chuckle to himself when the Road Runner would get over on Wile E. and say things like,

"That coyote never catches that bird. You'd think he'd eventually give up and try something else."

Then, my older brother or one of my cousins would laugh, but not at the cartoon. We'd be laughing at my grandpa, and he would think we were just laughing with him.

He used to take us grandkids fishing, hunting, or just shooting out on the desert east of Bend whenever we'd ask.

One time, one of my cousins and I went deer hunting with him when we were about 11 before we were able to hunt big game ourselves. Even though you had to be 12 in order to shoot a big game, we liked to go with him just to learn his habits in hopes of being as successful of a hunter as he was one day. He made us walk at the same time as he did, stepping into the same place that had just stepped in. In a single file line, we slowly made our way through the thicket, staying as close together as possible. About every two or three steps, he would stop, look up, and check to see if there were any deer around. He took his time, making as little noise as possible with every step he took. About halfway through our trek, he stopped and let out this long and noisy fart that seemed to echo throughout the whole forest. Well, I was about two feet away from his butt when he let loose, and I got the full force of the stink bomb right in my face. As I started waving my hands back and forth, trying to disperse the foul smell that lingered in the air for what seemed to be an eternity, I turned around and looked at my cousin for help. When we made eye contact, we couldn't help but start to laugh at the situation that was now engulfing him as well. No sooner than we started laughing, trying to keep as quit as we could, grandpa turned around without saying anything and gave us both a glaring look that we understood meant that we needed to immediately stop making noise. Though this was a pretty tall order for two little boys, we managed to control ourselves, plug our noses, and continue on with the hunt.

Though we got nothing that day, we enjoyed just being out in the woods hanging out with those we considered to not only be one of the greatest hunters on the planet but probably the greatest men we would ever have the privilege of knowing. Even as children, we knew that our Grandpa Warren was like no other man we had ever been around or would probably ever be. Being a grandpa now myself, I find it easy to look back at the way he loved his family and draw from the well that he once built. He was never too busy to be there, always ready to be there for his family no matter what the needed. Whether it was something to eat when you walked in the front door or leaving a sleeping bag on the front porch in the winter. As we got older, he knew some of his grandchildren were out running around in the streets, and would probably need something warm to sleep in on nights we wouldn't make it back home. At 56 years old, I still consider him the greatest man I have ever known.

I was fortunate enough to have known two grandpa's in my life. Even though, as a child, I spent more time with my grandpa Warren because he and my grandma lived in Bend, I was able to spend more time with my mom's parents the older I got. My Granddad and Grandma Turner had a farm in Washougal, WA, that I was able to spend time on with them as well.

One summer in between my freshman and sophomore year of high school, I worked on my Granddad and Grandma Turner's farm, picking tansy out of the hay fields. Due to the fact that they're poisonous for livestock to eat and can't be mixed in with the bales of hay come harvest time, they had to be handpicked. They had over twenty acres of land, so this took several days of walking through the fields with a burlap bag, just pulling them out of the ground with my glove-covered hands. My granddad was right out there with me, making sure I didn't miss any, spending all day meticulously clearing out each of the two fields they had.

After clearing the fields of all the poisonous weeds, granddad set me to fill up the wood shed that was just off the back porch. They needed quite a bit of wood due to the fact that the wood-burning cook stove in the kitchen was the only source of heat for the old small 2-bedroom farmhouse they had. He started up the old Ford tractor, hitched up a two-wheeled utility trailer he had, and instructed me to drive up the back field until I came to a huge pile of wood that had already been cut up into pieces that would fit into the stove. He told me that when I got to a certain spot in the field, he wanted me to back up the trailer until I reached the woodpile. If you've never had the opportunity to back up a two-wheeled trailer with a tractor, then you don't know what you're missing in life. This is no simple task and is probably the hardest way to learn how to develop one's skill of backing up anything. I struggled to keep the trailer directly behind the tractor, as it would always end up going completely sideways and either to the left or the right. I figured out how to just pull straight-up catawampus to the woodpile without backing up. I caught granddad heading out towards the wood pile with a disappointed look on his face and shouting out some instructions that I couldn't understand until I had shut the tractor off. When he finally got close enough to hear, he said in a gruff voice,

"I told you I wanted you to backup that trailer up when you got to the wide spot I made for you. Why aren't you doing like I told you how to do it? "

I responded, "Well, it's too hard because the trailer just ends up going sideways before I can get close enough to the woodpile, and I'm wasting too much time trying to figure it out."

He said, "I don't care about how much time it's taking you. We got all summer for you to fill that woodshed up, and I want you to learn how to back this rig up the right way."

I took a deep breath, shook my head in agreement with a verbal yes, and continued to struggle until I had finally mastered the art of backing up a two-wheeled trailer with an old farm tractor.

After I had finished my chores for the day, I was greeted back at the house by both my grandma and granddad, brimming ear to hear with proud smiles on their faces and giving me hugs and accolades for my accomplishment for the day.

Grandma says, "I'm so proud of you, Michael. I watched you through the window as you struggled, so I didn't want to go outside and make you any more nervous than you already were. I could see you getting a little frustrated with yourself, but look at you now; great job."

Granddad chimed in, "Yea, I could see a little bit of your dad's temper coming out in you as you were gettn' it down. Good job for sticking with it and figuring it out. That's something you'll take with you the rest of your life and be proud of."

As my reward for helping out that summer, they took me down to Sears and bought me some new cloths I was going to need for the school year. They also took me to the Clark County Fair over in Ridgefield, and we spent the day eating our way around the grounds until it was time for the concert to start. And the artist who was performing that night was no other than the incomparable Johnny Cash. They hadn't told me about the concert until we got there, so it was a big surprise for me to be able to see the Man in Black up close and personal as he played all of his biggest hits. We were only a couple of rows away from the stage, so I was able to see all of the expressions on his face as he belted out the timeless classics that I had heard so many times on the radio before. This was the first concert I had ever been to, and what a concert it was. This was Johnny freaking Cash, man, the one and only Man in Black. I was in heaven, and I never wanted that concert to end. I just wanted to stand there as I banged my head in the air to songs like Walk the Line and Folsom Prison Blues. How could life get any better than where I was at that moment in time? I was with two people whom I greatly adored and respected, listening to and watching one of the greatest artists that music would ever have to offer. I knew exactly where I was and what I was getting to experience in life. I was so grateful for what my grandparents had given me that summer, not just the clothes and the concert that they had given me, but the feeling of being loved that can only be experienced by what grandparents can give someone.

 As I lay there in my bed that evening after calling it a day and returning to the farm, I remember feeling like I just wanted to stay there with them forever and never leave that farm. I reflected on all the things I had done and learned. I thought about how I could not only take care of all the chores that the farm would require but that I could take care of them as they got older. I fell asleep dreaming about how perfect that summer was and how it was exactly the way I wanted to spend the rest of my life. But just like all good things that must finally come to an end, I found myself setting in the front seat of their car as granddad drove me back to Longview so I could start attending my second High School in as many years. What a bummer.

Chapter IV

By the time I was 15, I had been lifting weights for a few years and regained some of the confidence that had been taken away from me when I was younger, but it was also replaced with an anger that would spiral me into a world of drugs and alcohol that temporally filled the void that was created within me.

I had already been smoking pot for a few years now, so making new friends came easier as I drifted off into a subculture where people found common ground just simply because they didn't fit in with the normalities of life. I found other people who had similar experiences that I had, and we just seemed to click. I began to view life as an impossible journey to accomplish without the relief of mind-altering substances that would allow me to forget about the mental anguish that was so embedded into my soul that I had thought it would never go away. And as the old saying goes, "Misery loves company."

I moved back to Bend after my sophomore year and got a job washing dishes at a local restaurant.

With the help of my father, I bought a motorcycle as my first vehicle. When I would ride that Kawasaki KZ-440 around, it was as if I were my own king. No drink or drug could compare to the feeling I had while being on the road in charge of my own destiny. Just the simple task of deciding which root I was going to take in order to get to my destination gave me a sense of freedom like no other. I could go anywhere at any time I wanted to, and ultimately, no one could stop me. Just the thought of having the option of riding off into the sunset was soothing to my soul, and I took advantage of it every chance I got.

One time, after getting mad at my dad for some unknown reason, I went home, packed my bags, and rode from Bend, OR, back up to my grandparents' farm in Washougal, WA. After spending a few days with them, I ended up back at my mom's in Longview, WA, starting over once again. I didn't have a map, so I just rode from the memories I had when we used to visit them on holidays and sometimes in the summer. At 16, I felt like I was unstoppable from doing whatever I wanted to do. My motorcycle was my ship, and I was the captain. While in Longview, I just hooked back up with the old crowd I used to hang around and started the cycle of getting into trouble all over again. This time, I ended up needing my mom to pick me up from jail a few times. I never had to stay the night; they would just book me and then make me call my mom to go down and pick me up. Fighting and drinking in public were the usual crimes of the day.

One time, a friend and I were partying at the house that was a few miles out of town, and we ran out of beer, so we decided to hop on my motorcycle and cruise back into town for another half rack even though it was raining. On our way back out to the party, we were making our way along this winding back country road that had some pretty sharp corners, and I was pushing the limits of my abilities to stay on the road. As I was navigating my motorcycle at speeds higher than I should have been, we came up on this sweeping left-hand corner that I thought I could make no problem. But due to the fact it was raining and the road was slippery, I misjudged the extent of what I was facing. We ended up riding the shoulder down into a ditch full of soft gravel that slowed us down some, but as we came to a driveway that crossed the ditch to the road, I realized we were running out of options. I made a quick decision to turn the motorcycle to the right, opposite the road, and hit both front and back breaks. This would end up sending both of us flying over the handle bars into a bunch of shrub bushes that almost acted like a trampoline and softened our fall. We stood up, picked up our half a case of beer, got back on my bike, and rode off. We were both amazed. We didn't even break one bottle; we thought it was a miracle. Not so much that we didn't die, but that we had saved all of the beer and had plenty for the rest of the night.

When you're a teenager, you feel like you're bulletproof, and you don't believe you're ever going to die, at least not when you're young. Dying is for old people who have already lived a full life and don't need to be around anymore, or so I thought.

After wrecking my motorcycle and with the encouragement of my mother, I went back to live with my dad in Bend and started attending my 3rd High School. Even though I knew she loved me, I was beginning to be much more than she and my step-dad Mike could handle. Even though Mike was a great guy and treated my mom well, I just didn't respect him as a father figure and continued to do whatever I wanted to. I had no fear of what the consequences would bring, so I continued to get into trouble without feeling accountable for my actions.

Once again, I would start making friends with the wrong crowd and continue my spiral back down into nothingness and darkness filled with partying and depravity. My dad was about to marry his 3rd wife, who was a Christian and used to drag us to church on Sundays. Even though I was hungover or still drunk, when we would go, I could feel something tugging at my heart that I didn't understand.

One Easter Sunday, while attending the morning service, the pastor preached on the crucifixion of Jesus Christ, which had me so attentive to what he was saying that I had lost all sense of where I was. As he began to explain what it's like physically to be crucified and what your body goes through before you die, I began to weep uncontrollably. I seemed to drift off into a foreign land and have a visualization of a man being nailed to a cross and what it must have been like to hang up there on it by only the metal spikes that had driven through his hands and feet. My eyes couldn't stop watering as the preacher described how one would not only experience the excruciating pain rushing through all points of their body but how one would also struggle to breathe as one began to suffocate due to their arms being stretched out and the weight of their body applying so much pressure to your chest causing asphyxiation allowing the relief of death to come. I couldn't understand why this depiction was so real to me. Why was this morning's service so different from all the other ones that I had been dragged to? Why couldn't I set still as he talked about every aspect of what it's like to be crucified? I had convinced myself that even if there was a God, which I didn't really believe there was, how could he have allowed me to go through all the pain and suffering that I had gone through in life as a little boy? How could a just and loving God put such an innocent child through so much humiliation and anguish that he didn't deserve? If he was so real, why wasn't he there for me when I needed him the most? So many thoughts and emotions were rushing through my mind and body that I didn't want to be there anymore. I just wanted to get up, walk outside, and walk home by myself. I knew if I did, I would never hear the end of it, so I sat there in silence, wiping the tears away from my eyes, trying to understand what was going on inside of me. I mean, before my parents got divorced, I went through CCD classes at the Catholic Church we attended, so it's not like I hadn't been to church before; it's not like I didn't have some kind of understanding of who God and Jesus were. So why was this trip to church so different from all the others?

When the service finally ended, and I was able to walk out with the family, even though I had a sense of relief, it was over; there was still something unsettled in my heart and mind. It wasn't until that summer that my world would be turned upside down once again.

Chapter V

In the summer after my junior year in High School, I made friends with a guy I was introduced to by my older brother, who was about 25 years old and already had a family. I started hanging around them on a regular basis, and partying became a regular occurrence as the summer months kicked in. I didn't have a job then, so I would fill up my time with partying and basically doing whatever I wanted to. By this time, my dad was pretty laid back with what I was allowed to do. I thought the rules were pretty easy to follow at first: #1, don't make him pick me up from jail; #2, if you're not home by midnight, the screen door gets locked, and you have to stay wherever I was. I was always hanging around people who were older than me because I just seemed to fit in with them more than kids my age, so they had either houses or apartments I could crash at. I was growing up faster than I should have been, and I enjoyed the perspective in life they had over the immature peers I ran into at school. Besides, they could buy hard alcohol more easily than I could. Even though back in the mid-'80s, it was pretty easy for me to buy beer due to the facial hair I could already grow, coupled with confidence, or cockiness as it were, and I could buy beer at just about any store I wanted to.

I spent the 4th of July with my new friends, partying and getting wasted, as usual, and stayed the night at their house. The next day, after we got up, we decided to go out in the desert and shoot some guns that we had and make a day of it. So we grabbed the guns and a half gallon of whiskey, and all of us, 5 adults and two children, pilled in their car and headed east. As we commenced shooting everything we came in contact with, we all took turns drinking straight out of the jug. We were all feeling pretty good by the time we ran out of ammo and started our return back home. Driving down the old Bend-Redmond Highway that was full of more twists and turns than my friend could eventually handle with too much whiskey in him, we finally fell victim to one corner that has since been straightened out due to how dangerous it was. With his wife nagging at him to slow down, he made the decision to speed up and try to pass a car that was too close to the corner. As he tried to get back in our lane before taking the corner, the back end of the car slid off into the dirt as he tried to maintain control. He was doing pretty good and almost got it back up on the road, but before he could, we hit a small bolder and flipped the car somewhere around 9 times. Prior to the wreck, I had been setting shotgun in the car all day long but decided to let one of the other guys who was with us set there. I couldn't believe I said yes when he asked me if he could ride shotgun back to our other friend's house, where we had just dropped the guns off. I would always set shotgun while riding out of pride, and I couldn't believe I let him take it. As we were driving down the road, I was still thinking about why I had let him in the front while I was in the back with our other friend and the baby in the car seat. After I woke up from being knocked out for what I was told to be about 20-30 minutes, I opened my eyes and could hear moaning in the front seat coming from my friend, the driver, who I later found out had broken his neck. As I set up and put my feet on the ground, due to the fact we had eventually landed right side up on all four tires, I could see the legs of the friend who I had let take the front seat sticking out from underneath the car. I looked under the car and saw what was left of his mangled body stuck between the ground and the car. The friend who was in the back seat with me was holding the baby and told me our other friend was dead. He told me he thought I was dead as well until I woke up. He told me he had pulled me off of the baby and positioned me on the back seat, and then waited for the driver's wife and their 5-year-old daughter, who both were in the front seat also, to return from walking to the nearest house and calling an ambulance. They said I probably saved the baby's life with the way that I was positioned on top of him in his car seat; it was as if I somehow had shielded him with my body.

The ambulance finally showed up with the wife and her daughter, and we all pilled in, except for the friend under the car. We started our long trip to the local hospital. I ended up with a severe concussion and a messed up back that still reminds me to this day of that fateful trip out in the desert. I had a hard time processing why I had let our friend ride in the front that day, and he ended up dying instead of me. I began to see life in a way that I didn't understand. I started questioning my very own existence and wanted to know why I was allowed to live that day and not the other guy. Why did I allow him to set in the front as I took the backseat? It was too much for me to process by myself, and I drifted even further into darkness. The people around me could see that I was different now, as I wasn't as cocky as I was before. I began to contemplate my own existence, trying to figure out what my life was made for.

As I continued my life of debauchery, I found myself going around to all the churches in Bend and talking with all the various pastors, clergymen, and priests who would talk with me. But they just told me the same thing: I needed to get a job and move on with my life. Well, that didn't sit very well with me as I had felt there had to be more to life than just living and dying. Even though my parents had told me the same thing, I just couldn't hang my hat on the idea that all there was to my life was getting a job, waiting to retire, and then dying. There had to be more to this life. I mean, why am I still alive and my friend dead?

Chapter VI

At 18 years old, while struggling to find my place in this world, I decided that the best thing I could do was join the military and not only serve my country but go off to a foreign land and fight off the tyranny that was spreading across our world. I didn't want some desk job of a boring life of working on some military base here in America; I wanted to go overseas and literally go hand-to-hand combat with really evil people of this world. I wanted to feel like I was going to make a difference in the way this world is sculpted at the hands of men. I wanted to make sure that this country stayed at the forefront of democracy and all that it represented for the rest of the world in seeing how, when good people are given a chance to be free, what can be accomplished.

So one morning, I got up out of bed, marched down my happy little self to the recruiter's office, and took the ASVAB test. After listening to my older brother tell me stories about his encounters with some of them in San Diego when he was in Naval boot camp, I decided that I wanted to be a member of the elite fighting forces of the Navy

SEAL. I thought, what better way to take out bad guys than to be trained to kill someone in 1000 different ways? At the time, I certainly had the attitude for it, and after taking the test, I found out that I could do just about any job that the Navy offered.

The recruiter sent me from Bend up to the MEPS station in Portland, and they did their physical and psychological evaluations on me to see if I was fit for service. I spent the night in a hotel room that they had provided for me, and the next morning, I walked over to the station with a group of other prospective recruits who had stayed there also. While we were all walking across the parking lot that separated into two buildings, I began to have a sense of what it was going to feel like when I would finally join my fellow countrymen somewhere else in the world in the heat of a battle. I started to visualize what we would encounter and how we would respond to the call that we were all answering. I hadn't even been accepted yet, but somehow, I was placing myself right in the middle of what I had seen in movies and on TV.

As we entered the station and began all the testing that would be required of us that day, we came to the hearing test portion and were funneled into what looked like a giant walk-in freezer. I already knew that I had hearing loss in both of my ears, but I could hear well enough that I didn't need the help of hearing aids, so I felt confident that I would pass the test with no problem. After struggling to hear some of the high-pitched tones, they made everyone else leave the box except for me. I knew this wasn't a good sign as one of the facilitators came up to me and gave me some advice on how to trick the machine. Unfortunately for me, the advice didn't work. As I came out of the freezer box and made eye contact with the woman who was administering the test, I saw a slight disappointing look on her face and asked her if I had passed. She told me that she wasn't allowed to give any of the results to anyone and that I would have to talk with the recruiter when I got back to my home town.

I was immediately put back on the next bus to Bend and contemplated my situation with every passing mile that we drove past. That was the longest 4 ½ hour ride I had ever had in my life up until that point. I kept going over all of the scenarios that I could possibly think of in my mind.

I went from telling myself that I had passed the test and thinking of the day that I would actually get to San Diego to succumbing to the idea that I didn't pass the test and the military wasn't going to accept me.

The next day after waking up, I went back down to the recruiter's officer in Bend and talked with the recruiter who had sent me to Portland. When I walked in the front door, I could see that same disappointing look on his face that I had seen on the face of the woman who administered the hearing test back in Portland. He told me to sit down so he could go over the results of all the testing that I had gone through. He saved the hearing portion of the results for the last and gave me all of the positive ones that I had passed first. When he got my hearing deficiencies, he told me that my hearing was so bad that he wouldn't even waste his time, or mine, on putting for a waiver for me. He told me that there was a threshold that the military used for determining whether or not someone could get in even if they didn't pass the initial testing process. He said that I was so outside of that number that it wouldn't be worth even trying. He told me that he got money for every person that he enlisted, so I should know that he really wanted to sign me and get that bonus. But he said that it just wasn't worth the time and I should start thinking about another career path. Being extremely mad at this point, I stood up out of my chair and told him not to come knocking on my door if a war ever broke out. He assured me that Uncle Sam would call all of the able-bodied people before they ever got to me.

I still didn't want to believe that I couldn't join some branch of the service, so I left that office and walked downtown Bend to the Army Reserve station and talked with them. When I walked in and began to talk with that recruiter, he asked me if I had already taken the ASVAB test. When I told him that I had and the test score that I had received, his eyes lit up like a Christmas tree in the wintertime; he asked where I had taken it, and I told him down at the Navy's office a couple of weeks prior. He began to get a puzzled look on his face and asked why I had changed my mind about the Navy. I told him the experience that I had as his shoulders dropped, and took a breath. He told me that they used the same testing as the rest of the military did and that if I hadn't passed it with the Navy, I wasn't going to be able to join the Army Reserve either.

He felt my pain and recommended that I go down to a local hearing place and take another test to see whether or not I had just had a bad day when I had taken the one in Portland. So I left his office, walked down to the hearing center, and had them administer another test the same day. I immediately took my results back to the recruiter just to have him do the same thing,

"Sorry, son, you will never join the military. Thanks for trying, though. Have a nice day."

I stormed out of his office and tried to walk off my anger as I headed back home to tell my dad the bad news. I was full of so much anger and frustration with God that day that I just wanted to explode on anyone or anything that would come across my path. Fortunately, as I put my key in the front door and unlocked it, I was able to make it home without running into any situations along the way. When the evening came, and they both got home from work, I told my dad and his wife what had transpired that day as we all sat there in dismay, wondering what the next step in my life would be.

I had really thought that this was going to be my calling in life and that my temperament would fit the military to a tee. My step-mom tried to assure me that God just had a different plan for me. I really didn't want to hear anything about it at this point. I just wanted to be mad and sulk in my disappointment with life. I didn't want to hear anything about how much life still had to offer me or how there was a reason that I wasn't able to join. I just wanted to stay mad and take out my aggression on whatever I chose to do in life.

Chapter VII

At 20 years old, I continued to struggle to find my purpose in life, and I found myself digressing until I ended up staying in the Salvation Army Mission shelter there in Bend. I was in such a deep depression that I was continually thinking of taking my own life just to end the agony of not being able to figure out what I was made for. Nothing and no one was able to ease the pain I had in my heart as I felt all alone even when surrounded by people who loved me. Holidays just seemed to be worse even though I was interacting with my family.

Then, one evening, while staying at the shelter, we had to attend a bible study on Wednesday nights in order to stay there. I don't even remember what the study was about, but something happened to me that night. As I sat in there in my derogated state of mind, I heard a voice that was so comforting and hopeful tell me,

"I love you. I love you just the way you are, but I have something better for your life if you would just follow me."

I was immediately filled with joy and happiness that I hadn't had in a long time. I couldn't believe the rush of emotions that was surging through my body and brain. I hadn't experienced this kind of happiness since I was a child living back in the woods with my family still together. I was instantly confident that there was a bigger purpose for my life, just like I had been thinking there was. The hope that I had in my heart now was like no other hope I had experienced before. It all started to make sense as to why I was alive; it was for him, God. The Holy Spirit opened my eyes and showed me that Jesus had died for my sins and wanted me to walk with him throughout eternity. All of the sermons, all of the talks, and all of the pondering that I had done finally made sense. Everything came together that night as I had found my purpose to walk with Jesus and tell others about him, too. I couldn't believe the joy I was experiencing at this simple understanding that had just been revealed to me.

The next day after leaving the mission, I walked over to a park and read Mathew, Mark, Luke and John out of the little pocket bible that they had given me the night before and waited for the mission office to open up so I could tell my aunt what Jesus had done for me.

While sitting in the mission office getting ready to tell my aunt about Jesus, a guy in his mid-twenties walked in and wanted to know where the shelter was. I offered to take him down to it, and we headed out the door. I saw this as an opportunity to witness the first person I met since coming to the Lord. As we got into his truck, I noticed a crucifix hanging from his review mirror and decided this would be a good opportunity to find out if he knew who Jesus was.

"So, I see you believe in God," I said with more of a question in mind.

"Yes, I do," David responded.

"Do you," he asked?

I said, "Why yes I do. I just met him last night at the shelter we're going to. And let me tell you about Jesus."

David sat there attentively, listening to my newfound relationship with Jesus and how he had talked to me, filling me with hope and acceptance. He wanted me to share that with him. I told him how he had given me a joy so overwhelming that I couldn't contain it. I told him about how God loves us so much that he sent his only son to die on the cross so that we could not only go to heaven but have a better life while we were still here on earth. I noticed a smile on his face that seemed to be hiding something that he wanted to share with me, so I gave him a chance to talk. He took his opportunity as we pulled up to our destination and began to share that he had met Jesus some years back and had felt that God had directed him to come to Bend. He felt that there was someone here that he needed to talk to and help them with what God had for their life. He pulled back a tarp that was over the top of his belongings in the bed of his truck, and as he was digging in one of the boxes, he pulled out a book and handed it to me.

He said, "I believe you're the one God sent me here to talk to. I believe God has so much more for your life than what you could ever imagine."

I immediately sensed in my spirit that what he was saying was, in fact, straight from the heart of God. He told me that I was definitely on the right path but that I needed more direction. I don't remember who the author of the book was or even the title, but I read that book over in just a couple of days, and it helped me gain more of a perspective on God that he wanted me to have.

Over the course of a couple of months, David told me that God had spoken to him, and he needed to take me to San Jose, California, and get involved with a ministry that he had been involved with. He told me that they had helped him turn his life around, and they had a recovery home down there that would accept anyone who wanted to get their life together and know more about God. I told him that I felt like this was, in fact, from the heart of God, and I wanted to go. I told him that I needed to go up to Longview, WA, and visit my mom and stepdad for the holidays, but that I returned to Bend after visiting them. I could tell he felt a sense of urgency and didn't want me to go, but what could he say other than have a great time and look me up when you get back?

While spending Thanksgiving in Longview, we were going through some old picture albums, and I came across an old picture of someone I had never met before. I asked my mom who the fellow was, and she told me it was a cousin of hers who lived in Milpitas, California and hadn't seen him in probably 30 years. He was a country music musician who used to travel around the country playing in a band. After finding out that he lived right next to San Jose, the wheels started turning in my head. I had just started writing Christian songs already and had aspirations of playing my music for God one day. So I asked my mom if she still had his phone number and if she would call him to find out if I could stay with him until I could hook up with this new ministry that I had found out about. She got up and went to her address book, looked him up, and called the old number. Much to her surprise, he answered the phone. After reminiscing about old times and doing a little catching up, she told him about my situation and asked if I could stay with him while getting involved with this new ministry. Much to our surprise, he said,

"Come on down, and we'll get you plugged in."

With an address in hand, I went back to Bend and tried to look up David, but he had disappeared. I looked for him everywhere I thought he could be, but he had vanished from my life as quickly as he showed up. I still felt like God wanted me to go to this new ministry, so I purchased a one-way bus ticket to San Jose and left my family for a new life in California.

When I finally showed up in San Jose, I was met by a jovial man standing outside the bus station who asked me,

"Are you Mike?"

I responded, "Yes, I am. Are you Billy Joe?"

After making our accountants, we got into his car and drove back to his house, where I stayed for the next three days as I got in touch with the new church I was headed to. Boy, was I in for a surprise?

Chapter VIII

All the churches I had been to at that point were your typical white conservative churches. Sing a couple of songs, give your money, listen to a sermon, and then go home. I hadn't even heard of the word Pentecostal, at least that I could remember. When I walked into the front door of the recovery home I was headed to, I could hear people crying and wailing. They were praying out loud and laying hands on one another. They were speaking loud in some weird language that I had never heard before, which had me freaked out a little bit. My cousin, who drove me there, asked if I was sure this was the place I wanted to be. Feeling like I didn't have any more options, I just said yes and decided to stay.

I would spend the next 10 months and turn 21 in what was referred to as The Men's Home, praying, reading the bible, and attending multiple daily bible studies, getting my mind and heart right with God. I wasn't physically addicted to anything anymore when I went in, but I needed God to help me deal with the mentality that I had developed over the years. I needed my brain to be washed in the blood of Jesus in a big way. Even though God had called me, and I had responded to his call, I still needed him to change my way of thinking that years of disappointments and failure in life had caused me.

The time that I spent in that Christian recovery home was the hardest 10 months of my life. Not only did I learn about God through reading his word, daily prayer, and bible studies, but I also learned that not everyone else there wanted to be a Christian. And even the ones who wanted to change were coming out of the same darkness that I was and struggled to be like Jesus, just like myself. I learned that as Jesus was patient with me, I, too, needed to be patient with those around me as well. Being a Christian was harder than I thought it would be. Not only did I have to keep up with the daily routine in life, but I needed to start emulating the love of Christ even when other people weren't willing to. This, I found out, would be a lifelong journey, not an overnight transformation like the salvation I had received. Not only was I learning to love and see myself the way God does, and still am, but loving other people the way he does is equally challenging, if not harder.

I found out that God is not looking for perfect people to join his kingdom but that he wants willing souls. Not only is he looking for people who are willing to spread the good news of the gospel of Jesus Christ, his son who came to die for our sins and set us free, but he is looking for people who are willing to change their mentality and conform to his ways, not the selfish ways of the world. I found out that this process would be a daily work in progress that would be filled with peaks and valleys. I found out that a prayer life, along with his word and constant submission to his Holy Spirit, would be the keys to a successful walk with him. Though no one is perfect, there needs to be a sign of change that everyone else can see along the way as well. Other people may not read the bible, but they will read your life and judge for themselves whether or not this Jesus that we speak of is real or not. Not everyone is going to have a supernatural experience with God and walk away from their old selves like I did. Sometimes, accepting salvation is a slow process for people, and they need to constantly see the love of God in others in order to have things finally click inside their brains. They say that salvation is a foot and a half away, the distance between your heart and your head. The Bible says to be transformed by the renewing of your mind, and that's what's going to help others see his love. The Bible also says that we are overcome by the blood of the lamb and the power of our testimony. These two things go hand in hand and are the basis for our walk with Christ. As I overcome the struggles of this life I'm able to show others that they can too. We can walk away from all of the things that the devil would use to keep us down and rely upon the strength that Jesus gave us when he willingly gave up his life on that cross. When he was struggling with his calling, he looked to his father to give him the strength to overcome this world and give us salvation.

While still at home, I learned how to worship God in spirit and in truth with my cheap acoustic guitar that I had arrived with, and I would spend hours just worshiping him on my own. Not only did I find out that the separation from others was important at times, but I was building my relationship with the Holy Spirit through personal communion with him. Before I graduated from home, I was allowed to join the worship team in the church, which I took very seriously.

My dad was still married to his Christian wife at the time, who bought me an electric guitar and amplifier package, mailed it to me, and I used it for the worship team at church on Sundays and Fridays. As I wrote more songs for Jesus, the pastor would allow me to play them after the worship services and before he would preach, and I would pour my heart out for everyone to see. My prayer was that God would use my songs to touch other people's lives the way he touched mine. The church had around 800 congregants at the time, and I had never played on a stage in front of people before, so this was definitely something that I was going to need God to help me with. I would pray that he would give me the strength and the courage to stand up and be bold for him. Even though they were songs that I had written myself, I've always had a bad memory, and I was afraid I would forget the words.

After already suffering multiple concussions by then, I found it hard to concentrate and remember things. Also, when I was less than two weeks old, my mother had gotten up in the middle of the night to feed me just to find me not breathing and had turned blue. Fortunately for me, my paternal grandparents had just driven from Bend down to Redding, CA, where I was born, to see their new grandchild. As my mom started screaming and woke up everyone in the house, including the friends of my parents that we were staying with, my grandmother instructed my mom to take me into the bathroom as she grabbed a blanket off the bed. She had my mom get into the bathtub while holding me as she put the blanket over the top of us and turned on the hot water. The steam that was created eventually caused me to start breathing again, and then they took us to the hospital. The emergency room doctor told my mom that she should thank her mother-in-law for saving her baby's life, as I wouldn't have survived the trip to the hospital without being resuscitated first.

Even though concentrating and memorizing things has always been a constant struggle for me, I would stand up there and sing my songs with the words written down on a piece of paper that I had placed on a stand. People would tell me how much they enjoyed my music and how God had touched their hearts while I was singing. This gave me the fuel I needed to continue writing and singing my songs for God.

I eventually took my talents into the studio and began recording my songs with other musicians. I immediately enjoyed watching the songs that I had spent so much time creating come to life at the hands of producers and other talented musicians. Even though I was inspired to play them live and watch God move in the church, being in the studio was so much more relaxing and less stressful.

The Home was a mix of other men and women who had either been to jail or prison multiple times or were on their way there. Some were either drug dealers or gang members who were trying to get out of lengthy prison sentences and show the judge that they were trying to change their lives by freely entering the program, while others were court-mandated and had no intention of ever-changing. The administrators even had me act as a court liaison for some of the men by explaining to their prospective judges what the recovery home entailed, thus trying to help them get out of their prison sentences. Some of the judges already knew about the Home and had no problem allowing them to return with me; others needed more convincing about what was happening, and I would explain the rigors of daily life while there. Some men would choose to go back to jail rather than stay in the Home and allow God to change them. They would say that prison or jail was easier to do their time in rather than be subjected to all the various rules one had to follow while being in the Home, and they were right.

One time, after bible study and only being in the Home for about a week, I ran upstairs in order to be the first one to take a shower. With around 70 men being in the Home at any given time, taking a shower with hot water was something I had not yet encountered. As I jumped in, turned on the precious hot water, and began to lather up, I heard a voice from one of the staff members ask,

"Who's timing you Mike?"

I responded, "No one."

I had forgotten that you had to be timed by someone when you got in the shower due to the fact that when the water was turned on, you had 3 minutes to get in and get out. I didn't even care at that point because I was so happy just to have hot water. The staff member says,

"You know you're going to get discipline now."

I responded with an F-bomb and didn't even care about the consequences as I let the warm water roll off of my head. In fact, I decided I might as well take a little more than my allotted 3 minutes due to the fact that I was already in trouble.

After I had gotten out, dried off and went back downstairs, I was handed a formal piece of paper with the bible verse Ephesians 4:29; "Don't allow any unwholesome talk come out of your mouths, but only what is helpful for building others up according to their needs, that it may benefit those who listen." It had X's-250 in one week written next to it, meaning that I had to write that verse 250 times in one week for my transgressions. Once again, I was so happy just to have received my first hot shower since arriving there that I didn't even care.

After spending 10 months in the home, I moved in with a family who attended the same church, got a job with Xerox, and started to assimilate into the big city way of life. This was no small task for this country boy to accomplish. Even though I had been around the people in the Home and introduced to the differences in the mentality we had, I wasn't out in the city making my own way.

The husband of the family that I moved in with was also a musician, so we would spend time worshiping God and playing songs for his family. We would also lead worship before the bible studies that we had at their house, as other people in the church who lived nearby would come over on Wednesday nights to socialize and get closer to God. I really enjoyed attending the bible studies because this is where I began to develop friendships with other people in the church. Getting to know one another during church was very limited as there was only so much time to talk to people, and then we had to leave. There was no time limit on the bible studies, and sometimes, we would spend hours after the initial study just fellowshipping and getting to know each other. We would share what was going on in each other's lives, good and bad. We would pray for each other, thanking God for the victories he had already given us and claiming the ones that we were in need of. I learned that the church is just one big extended family where everyone can turn to each other to share their experiences in life, no matter what they are going through. Up until that point, I had just thought that was what your natural family was for. But God was showing me that there was so much more to life than what I was used to.

I ended up getting a job at Xerox in Sunnyvale, and they would send me out to different businesses around the Bay area. I would drive all the way from South San Jose to downtown San Francisco, working in the perspective copy centers at various locations. Not only did I have to figure out where these places were, I had to hone my defensive driving skills just to get there. The Bay Area is a melting pot of people from just about every other country in the world. Not only did I have somewhat of a culture shock, these people did not know how to drive.

One time, on my way to a large law firm in San Francisco that was located in one of those skyscraper buildings that I had never been in before, this little old oriental man who was driving in the lane next to me on my left all of a sudden started coming over into my lane. He ended up hitting my front bumper with his back end, and we pulled over to the side of the freeway to assess the damage and talk. I noticed there wasn't any damage to speak of to my car or his, and then I asked him why he came over into my lane and hit me. In broken English with a heavy accent that I could barely understand, he said,

"I turn on my blinker."

I responded, "You do know that you have to check to see if anyone else is in the lane before you enter it, right?"

He retorted, "No. I turn on my blinker."

I explained, "Sir, yes, you do have to turn on your blinker first, but then you have to check to make sure no one else is in the lane before you enter it."

He retorted again, "No. I turn on my blinker."

I said, "Sir, do we need to call the police and have them come out and explain this to you? You can't just turn your blinker on and then drive wherever you want to. Doesn't that sound just a little bit dangerous?"

He looked at me as his face changed and said, "No, police. No police."

I said, "OK, no police. But you need to understand that you need to make sure that the lane is clear before you enter it. It's against the rules, and it's just not safe."

He shook his head, yes, and we both drove off and went on about our own ways. I was telling a fellow coworker who was from Vietnam about the story, and he said the old man more than likely got scared when I mentioned the police. He said in Vietnam, you never call the police for anything because most of them are corrupt and have a habit of beating people because most of them were a holdover from the communist regime that had once ruled there. I felt a little bad for the old man as I had probably brought back some old memories for him. I guess my coworker must have seen a change on my face and told me he was probably used to it and would be ok. I silently prayed for the old man and went back to work.

I really felt fortunate to work around so many different cultures and walks of life. Getting to know other people who had such a vast difference in their background and upbringing than I did was exciting to me. I worked with people from Africa,

India, Portugal, England, and, of course, California being a border state, Mexico. I can't remember all of the different countries that everyone came from, but I set out to try all the different foods that they would tell me about as we spent our days making copies and getting to know one another. Not only did I enjoy hearing about their life experiences, it helped me step outside of myself and see life in a different way. There was not much in the way of world culture coming from small-town America. There was only one black family in Bend when I grew up there. They had two boys who went to my school, and I ended up making friends with the one who was my age when I was 10. There was also only one Hispanic family who had a boy who was my age, but we went to different schools, so we never hung around each other until I was about 18. And that was it.

I got involved in several different ministries while attending the church. On top of playing the guitar at Fridays' and Sundays' worship services, I was asked if I wanted to go help out at the bible study in California Youth Authority in Stockton on Thursday nights. When I went there back in 1990, they housed children from the age of 9-24. We provided bible studies to the 16-17-year-olds every week.

After about 6 months of helping out, the leader asked me if I wanted to take it over as he had been asked to take over another ministry in the church. This was the first time I had ever been asked to lead a ministry by myself, and I accepted the call. We only had about 10 kids who would show up when I first started helping out, but about 4-5 months after I had taken it over, there were about 50 kids who were regularly attending the study. After the study was over, I would stay and talk to them one-on-one and get to know them personally. I would pray and talk with them and encourage them that this wasn't the end of their lives. I would assure them that this wasn't the end of the road for them. I would try to help them understand that God still had so much more for them and that he still loved them no matter what they had done with their lives so far. Teaching them love, forgiveness and hope. I gave my life as a testimony that God has not given up on them, no matter how far down the road they have gone. He still loved them just the way they were and had a better life for them if they would just surrender to his love.

After about a year and a half of driving back and forth to Stockton every Thursday night after work, the pastor asked me if I wanted to take over the preteen ministry. He told me that he had heard about how God had been blessing the Youth prison ministry I was doing, and he felt that I could do the same with the children.

Now, I was single at the time and didn't have any children to fall back on as experience to draw from. I looked at him in bewilderment and thought, is this guy crazy? How am I going to be able to handle a bunch of 9-12 year kids? I guess it was written all over my face because he chuckled and said,

"Don't worry about it, Mike. Just like God was with you in the prison ministry, he will be with you in this ministry also."

I accepted the challenge and started that next Friday, and man was I in for a surprise. After spending most of the service just trying to calm the kids down and stop them from running around the classroom and yelling, I went home with a headache the size of California.

I spent the next three years learning how to teach children the way that they needed to be taught. I spent countless hours praying and talking to God about what and how he wanted me to teach them. Even though I preached and taught them the bible, the biggest thing I found myself doing was just being their friend. Everything from being there for them when their parents were in the hospital to taking them jet skiing and to the movies. Watching them grow older and move on to the youth group was a very happy yet sad time for me.

After about 3 years of watching over the children, the pastor invited me out to their house to have lunch with his family and told me how appreciative he was that I had helped organize that ministry. He told me that he wanted to turn it over to the couple that had been assisting me for the last year or so. He could tell that I was very attached to what I was doing and didn't want to give it up, but he assured me that God was just taking me into a new season. We drove down to the music store, and he bought a new pair of guitar strings that his wife needed for her guitar. When we returned, I changed out the strings, and we worshipped God together, just thanking him for his faithfulness and goodness. He told me this was a time for me to return to the worship team and just receive from God. He knew how much I had given of myself over the last 3 years and that this was a season for me to just focus on God and receive.

Chapter IX

After spending 7 years in San Jose, almost to the day, I decided it was time for me to move back to Oregon and start my life over again. I really enjoyed the ministry that I had been involved in that was worldwide, so I looked at the address of a sister church that was in Portland and went to visit the pastor to see how it was. The first time I walked through the doors of the sanctuary, I saw these two women cleaning the church and walked up to ask them if they knew where the pastor was. They told me he was just down the sidewalk in the same building inside of his office. They told me they were his sisters and asked me who I was. Little did I know at the time I would end up marrying the younger one named Carmina.

After meeting the pastor, I decided that I would make this my new home church, and I started to get involved there as well. After telling the pastor that I had led worship at the previous I had been involved with, he asked me if I would be interested in getting involved with his worship team. I agreed and started to assimilate with my new church family.

One day, after attending church for a couple of months, Carmina came up to me after church and said she was collecting the names and phone numbers of all the singles in the church and wanted to know if I wanted to give mine. You know, just so we could all stay connected and be there for each other. I thought it was a little suspicious, but I gave her mine, and we went on about our business. It only took a couple of days, and my phone rang.

I answered, "Hello, this is Mike."

This was in 1995, before I had a cellphone or caller I.D. so I had no inclination of who this might be. I heard what I thought was a familiar on the other end say,

"Hello, Mike. This is Carmina from the church."

I immediately thought to myself, I knew this was a setup. I responded by asking how she was doing and what was going on? She told me that the singles were getting together and wanted to know if I was interested in getting together for a movie and pizza night at one of the other singles' houses on Wednesday night. I should be sure. We talked for just a couple more minutes and hung up. I said to myself, that was pretty slick what she just put together.

When Wednesday rolled around and I showed up for singles night, I had a feeling that things were not as they seemed. While Carmina and her friend were dishing up the pizza, they fumbled the handoff with one of the plates and it went crashing down on the kitchen floor. I said to myself this would be a good opportunity to see the character of these two women. I had my eye on both of them at church, and I was just paying attention to how they both acted in different situations. One can never be too careful was my motto while searching for a spouse. Her friend immediately blamed Carmina for letting go of the plate before she had a hold of it, while Carmina said,

'Well, let's just clean it up. There's no sense in crying over spilt milk."

As she picked up a broom and cleaned up the mess. I said to myself, I think Carmina may have the character that I'm looking for.

Carmina continued to invite me to singles events, and within about three months, I had decided that I wanted to make her my wife. I figured that I had seen enough of her character and we should spend the rest of our lives together. At 28, I already knew what I liked and didn't like in a woman, and I liked her. She was out of town down at her parents' house visiting in California, where she was raised, and when she called me one night, I told her I was going to marry her. She laughed and exclaimed,

"Oh, really. How do you think you're going to do that?

I said, "Well, when you get back, I'm going to marry you. You're going to be my bride, and I'm going to be your husband."

She played coy and said,

"You know I have a 14-year-old boy at home?"

I said, "Yeah, I remember, his name is Gilbert. We were all just hanging out together before you left a couple of days ago."

She laughed it off and said,

"Well, we'll see about that when I get back."

I assured her that this was, in fact, going to happen, and we hung up the phone.

When she returned from her trip, we got together, and she told me that if we were, in fact, going to get married, she wanted a proper proposal. So I got down on one knee in front of her son and asked her to marry me. She said yes, and after about 7 months of dating, and 5 months later, on July 14th, 1996, I stole my fiancé from the rest of the world.

One evening, after we had gotten engaged while driving north on the I-205 in Portland, I was taking Carmina back home after we had just gone to dinner with several of my family members. I remember feeling like I didn't want the night to come to an end yet, and before we were able to reach her exit, Carmina said she was feeling the same way and asked me if we could just continue to drive around the city for a while. I said no problem, and we took the I-84 exit west and continued to extend our evening of just talking and enjoying each other's company. As we continued to drive around, extending our evening on the freeway, the lights from the city seemed to be shining like they had never shined before. The street lights, along with all of the businesses and houses we passed, seemed to be beaming and radiating colors that I had never seen before. As I looked over at Carmina and told her what I was experiencing, she had a bewildered look on her face and told me she was seeing the same thing. As she sat there mesmerized by what was happening, she asked me why the lights were different that night. I told her I had no idea but that it was really awesome as we continued to enjoy what was an ending to our already perfect evening.

When we finally did make it to her apartment after extending our date for about another half an hour, we still didn't want the night to end. I gave her a kiss on her doorstep and then drove back to where I was living in Oregon City. As I continued on my 35-minute drive back home, I knew that I was making the right decision to make this woman my wife.

When our special day did finally come, watching my beautiful bride being walked down the aisle by her father gave me an overwhelming sense of not only accomplishment and fulfillment but a sense of pride that I had found the perfect woman for me. As of the writing of this book, we've been married for 27 years, and what an adventure that has been. Our marriage hasn't always been as perfect as I thought it was going to be, and without going into any details, I would just say that if you want to learn how to argue, get married. If you want a black belt in arguing, get married to a spicy Latina. And at this point, that's all I'll say about that subject matter: I love you, Mamacita.

Carmina already had three children, two of whom were adults and lived in Central Washington at the time, and her youngest, who was 14 when we got married. The youngest decided to move to his father's to be around his brothers and the freedom that he didn't have with us, so he left shortly after we got married, leaving just the two of us to continue on our journey. We decided that we would try to adopt a little girl and expand our family the winter after we said our vows and bring some more happiness into our lives.

We decided that due to the amount of children that we knew who were in the state foster care system, we would pursue adopting a child from the state. We made contact with both the states of Washington and Oregon due to the fact that we lived in Camas, Washington, which is just right across the Columbia River from Portland, Oregon.

The close proximity made it easier to attend classes with both agencies that were required for anyone seeking to adopt a child out of their systems. After explaining our plan to both agencies, they both told us that was common practice among prospective parents and that they had no problem with us seeking to adopt out of either state.

After several months of attending weekly classes, it became clear that neither state had any good intentions of allowing us to take a child out of their systems. As the weeks dragged on without either state introducing us to even one child, we found out that they were more interested in us providing respite care over the weekends to their foster parents, who were supposed to be giving temporary homes for the children with no intentions of adopting them out. I found out that not only is this a money-making scheme for the states, but that there is a lot of nefarious activity involved as well. Those poor children are nothing more than a commodity for the states once they enter the system, and they have no intention of letting go of their cash cows. Once a child leaves their system, they can no longer make money off of them with their already bloated budgets. They see nothing more than dollar signs on top of every head they take in and plan on keeping them as long as they can. They move the children around from one foster house to the next their whole childhood, hiding them away from potential parents so as to keep the money rolling in off of each one they have in their so-called care. After about a year and a half of jumping through their hoops and attending more classes, we found ourselves not getting any closer to adopting a child, so we decided that we would give up on our dream of adopting a little girl who felt we had so much love to offer. Carmina wanted me to have the experience of being a father and offered to have her tubes untied, but I felt that at her age, it was too risky, and she wasn't willing to put her life in danger and take a chance on losing her. I had succumbed to the notion that one day, her children would have babies, and I would just jump straight to being a grandpa and bypass being a daddy.

As the years rolled on, my hopes of being a grandpa came true. And so far, we have been blessed with 7 grandchildren from her kids and two more coming from my nephew Jesse, who I see as a son. I will not say that I feel fulfilled without raising my own child, but I will say that the joy of being called grandpa and Uncle Mike is one of the most wonderful feelings that I have ever experienced in my life. I enjoy every minute that I get to spend with them when they are around, and I think about them all the time when they are not.

Chapter X

After 3 years of renting a house in Camas, we were able to buy our own home in the neighboring city of Vancouver, Washington. We had to put offers down on 3 other houses before we were able to finally purchase our dream home. For one reason or the other, all the deals fell through, leaving us empty-handed in the end. When we finally unlocked the door and entered our new home with feelings of elation, there was also a sense of relief, as we had been on the path to homeownership for over a year.

When we got our finances back in order, I took the opportunity to seek out a new music studio and producer to continue my dream of recording more of my music. In 2002, I recorded an 8-song CD titled The One Who Stays at a studio in Oregon City. Carmina and I were so proud that I was able to realize my dream of continuing to record my music and bring life to the songs that I had worked so hard at writing. In the past, I hadn't been able to record more than one song at a time, so when I recorded an 8 song CD, it was pretty special. The music producer that I used introduced me to a graphic arts designer who took some pictures that I had given her and created the jacket and sleeve. I went online and found a company that made professional copies and stamped the CDs so as to make everything look as palatable as possible. I shopped it around to a few record companies and made contact with some local radio stations, but I wasn't able to garner any attention from it. I thought for sure that the Christian radio station would be interested in playing at least one of the songs on the CD, but they told me it wasn't their kind of music and left me feeling dejected. I couldn't even get a country station to spin my CD in their local-only format. So I just continued playing my songs in church and ended up giving away more copies than I had sold.

Then, in 2004, I found a music producer in Nashville, TN, and Carmina and I headed out to the country capital of the world and spent 3 days in another studio recording 10 more songs. All of the musicians had major qualifications and were exactly what I was looking for to bring life to my next project. One was a resident player at The Grand Ole Opry, and all of them had toured with various country artists of the day. For example,

Garth Brooks used to record his demos with them that he would, in turn, pitch to the record companies before he made it big. Joe Nichols had also previously recorded some of his songs there as well. So, I felt confident that they were going to be able to put the flavor to the songs that I was looking for.

Three days in the studio doesn't seem like a long time to be able to record 10 songs, and it isn't. They had no problem creating their instrumental parts in a day and a half, but that left me with just a day and a half to do all the lead vocals. This I found this to be more challenging than I had initially anticipated. After powering through 8 hours of pushing my voice to the limit one day, we completed the project in 4 hours the next. After wrapping things up in the studio, the producer and his wife, who sang the backup vocals for me, took us to the airport, and we flew to Vancouver. Carmina wasn't happy with a female's voice being used to back me up. She thought it would have been better to use a stronger voice associated with a man's, like what was used on my previous project, but I thought it was fine as she had a great voice.

Once we got the copies back from the duplication company that we used to do the graphic arts and packaging, I started playing everywhere I could think of. I played my music in taverns and singing competitions all over the country. We traveled to Florida for one competition that winter and to Las Vegas for another. The competition in Vegas was televised on the USA network, so I got some national attention on that one. While performing at the local level of the Colgate Country Showdown in Roy, Washington, I lost to a local guy who forgot the words to a cover song he sang. He butchered "Hell Yeah" by Montgomery-Gentry, and I thought I was going to win and move on to the next stage of the competition that was scheduled to be held at the Washington State Fair in Puyallup. But as I found out, there was no way that the locals, who he was either related to or were friends of, were going to allow me to take that drive to the next level. They were going to vote for that guy no matter how good I was. I was supposed to get extra points for playing my guitar and performing an original song, but it made no difference. Not only could he not sing, he forgot the words to the cover song he destroyed; such is life. After years of performing and not getting any attention that would allow me to make a career out of my music, I decided to focus on making money the old-fashioned way, manual labor.

Chapter XI

After spending several years in the construction trade, I decided to try and get a job with the Oregon Department of Corrections. I went online, filled out all the necessary paperwork, and took a required test that would determine one's perceived qualifications for the job. Some people went to school to make themselves more prepared for the tests and interviews that would follow, but I thought I would give my hand a try at doing it without paying that extra money that we couldn't afford. Much to my surprise, I scored high enough on the test to garner my first interview with a prison.

A couple of weeks later, I received a letter in the mail offering me a chance to call Coffee Creek Correctional Institution in Wilsonville, Oregon and schedule my first of three interviews with them. After completing my first interview, I felt confident that things were progressing well, and that I would one day I would be a Correctional Officer. After my second interview, I was so confident that this was the direction God was leading me in that when I was at home, I received a call from a Lieutenant at the prison who wanted to ask me a few questions. I pulled off to the side of the road so I could concentrate on the questions he was going to ask, and we proceeded. I only remember one of the ten questions he asked as I made him laugh with my response. He asked me what I perceived to be my greatest weakness to be. I thought about some advice a retired Portland Police Officer and current US Marshall, who worked in the same building as I did in downtown Portland, had given me a few weeks before. He told me not to get too deep into my answers and to keep as light as possible while still staying professional with my responses.

I responded to the question with, "Cheeseburgers. I would say my greatest weakness is a good cheeseburger. I will drive miles for a quality burger on any given day."

After what seemed like an hour of silence, which had me questioning whether or not I had made the right decision, he started laughing and said,

"That's a pretty good response. I've never heard of anyone responding like that before in an interview."

As my confidence returned, I asked him if he would like a more solid answer than that one. He told me no and said that was a perfectly fine answer, and we moved on.

Feeling even more confident after we hung up, I received a job offer from the prison a few weeks later and started my new career as a Correctional Officer on the 6th of March, 2006.

While back in California, I got involved with the prison ministry at my previous church, so this wasn't the first time I had been inside a prison. I had been to Vacaville Prison, led worship, and spoke at the services that a group of us from the church had done a couple of times. I had also taken over a weekly bible study at the California Youth Authority in Stockton, driving every Wednesday after work from San Jose to Stockton and getting back home around 10 o'clock in the evening, so I wasn't my first time being inside a prison. But also wasn't the enemy back then, as I was bringing hope to the inmates, and didn't have a target on my back like I did now.

I will admit the first time I walked into one of the celled units on the male intake side of Coffee

Creek, and a whole tier of 26 metal doors slammed shut at once and rang out in an almost deafening manner, chills ran up and down my spine, and every hair stood up on my body at the same time. I won't say that I questioned the validity of the decision I had made to be there, but it most certainly gave me pause to put things into perspective of where I was and the responsibility that was now laid before me. Even though I took my job seriously, I always tried to bring some humor and understanding with me every day that I was there, some days being harder than others. I just tried to be myself and help those who wanted help. I learned that some people want your help, while some people want to be left alone. And then there is 1% who wanted to try and make your job as hard as they can; I had no problem facilitating all three. I know I helped out way more than I had sent to segregation, so I left with a sense of accomplishment when I had left. Even when I did place an individual in segregation, I knew they had earned it and had no problem with the decision they had made. I was just fulfilling their wishes to be separated from the rest of the population.

One time, while working in the male intake side, I saw the fact that not only was this Oregon's female prison but it was also used to temporarily house all of the men who had just left their county jails being sentenced. While we were waiting for them to complete their assessments and be transferred to their respective prisons, I had a situation where two gang members jumped one rival gang member just outside of one of the housing units in a corridor. As I jumped in to break up the fight while two other officers just stood there watching beat down, one of the inmates turned on me and tried to put me in a headlock. I was able to escape it before he could secure his hold, and I slammed him to the concrete floor and put him in a sleeper hold. Understanding that I was now in control of the situation, he relaxed his body and submitted to me before he passed out, so I released the hold and handcuffed him as we lay on the ground.

I would spend the next 10 months at home recovering from surgery on my wrist that was required due to the fact that when I took him down, we both landed on my right hand that was under his body. Fortunately, that was the only time I was assaulted during my 7-year career. After being diagnosed with Meniere's disease in October of 2010, it progressively got worse as I battled bouts of vertigo for 3 years until my doctor finally placed me on permanent disability in February 2013. It was a little scary entering the world of not being able to work anymore, but I just trusted God that he was going to provide for us and see us through whatever would come our way, which he always has.

Chapter XII

After my best friend Tim, who was living with us at the time, passed away, we decided to move away from the rain-drenched area we were living in and go to a dryer climate. The research that I had done on Meniere's disease suggested that a more stable weather environment that didn't have as many barometric pressure changes as the Vancouver area had might be easier on my body. So, after months of praying and asking God what he thought, I decided that we should move over the mountains to sunny Yakima, WA. Carmina's children and the grandkids, along with two of her sisters and their families, lived there, so we thought that it made good sense to pack up and see what God had east of the Cascades. Carmina's job allowed her to transfer, so it was fairly easy for us to make the transition. We put our house up for sale and made the move to Yakima in February 2015. After spending 2 months with her youngest son and his family, in April, we moved into our new home.

Carmina ended up retiring 2 years later, thus giving us all the time in the world to spend with all the family who we were around now. My parents had moved away from being within an hour's drive either north or south from our home in Vancouver, with my mom and stepdad moving to Arizona and my dad moving back over to Central Oregon, giving us an opportunity to be around more family and take care of grandchildren.

Our life was now filled with family stopping by on any given day of the week and weekends full of BBQs and family gatherings. We're all Seahawk fans, so when football season rolls around, we pick a house to gather in and root for the home team. Holidays are always filled with family getting together and enjoying the company of the simple things in life. Even though my body limits me to the activities I can be involved in now, just the simple act of either having a sister-in-law stop by and visit for a few hours or babysit any of our beautiful grandchildren warms the innermost being of my heart.

We struggled to find a new home church after moving, but after 8 years of searching and asking God to lead us to a new church family, we came in contact with a ministry called Breakthrough Church. From the first time we walked in the door and worshiped God in the sanctuary, I felt the spirit of the Lord moving in a special way there. I began to break down and cry during the first service we attended there like I hadn't done in many years gone by. I felt that God had, in fact, brought us to this new ministry to not only worship in song with his people but also to feel that he still had a purpose and calling on my life that I had begun to think had left me.

After being disabled, I succumbed to the way of thinking that God couldn't use me in the way he had used me before. I felt that I was now destined to just be around my family and focus on them. I didn't feel like my music had any more purpose other than just me playing and writing my songs in the spare room of our house and then leaving them there, mainly for God to hear. I didn't feel like God could use me in the same capacity as he once did when I was leading worship and playing my songs all over the country. I had simply succumbed to the lie that we were going to move on to our next destination and wait on the Lord to take me home and spend the rest of eternity with Jesus.

In 2023, prior to listening to Pastors Brian and Kari Jennings preach about what God wants to do not only in us but also through us, I started feeling a renewed sense of God calling me to draw closer to him. I started to feel like God did have more that he wanted me to accomplish in life than just spending time with my family and waiting around to die. Everything that was being preached behind the new pulpit that we had been led to was right in line with what God had already been dealing with deep inside my soul. The Holy Spirit began renewing my mind and filling my spirit with a new fire for God that I had once had in years gone by. Even though I had continued to talk and pray to God, my spiritual life had taken a nosedive over the years as I allowed the disappointments in life to get the better of me instead of giving God my best.

Even my prayers had now begun to change as I sought God. I wasn't just praying for my family and asking for God to meet my needs anymore, but I was asking him to renew my mind and create a right spirit within me. In Joshua 1:9, God tells us,

"Have I not commanded thee? Be strong and of good courage; be not afraid, neither be thou dismayed; for the Lord thy God is with thee whithersoever thou goest."

This scripture was given to me the first week I entered the Men's Home back in San Jose back in the beginning of 1989 when the Home director set me down one day as I was contemplating whether or not I had made the right decision to move there. I was debating whether or not I wanted to continue to subject myself to all the new things that I was encountering that were stretching me in ways I had never been stretched before. It really gave me not only a sense of encouragement, but also a greater understanding that God would always be with me no matter where I was. Not only was this a source of hope for my future, it was an outright command from God. The scripture was not just some suggestion that God had for me; it was exactly the way he wanted me to live my life, no matter where I am or what I'm doing.

As I sit here writing this book, I still continue to be filled with thoughts of what not only God has for me but also of the personal relationship that he wants to have with me on a daily basis. My friendship with the Holy Spirit that I had once allowed to wane has not only been renewed, but it has taken on a new meaning for me. In allowing my relationship with God's spirit to take a backseat, I had lost what his purpose for my life was. As I continue to focus on the relationship that he wants to have with me, the friendship that he so desires to have with me has taken on a new light. Scriptures like the one found in Mathew 6:33, "Seek ye first the kingdom of God, and his righteousness; and all these things shall be added unto you," have taken on a new meaning for me.

Even though I've known this scripture for 35 years, he has given me a renewed sense of what it really means. Asking the Holy Spirit to walk with me and search my heart all day, every day, has helped me to understand that the relationship that he desires to have with us is so much more important than anything we could ever do for him. Coming into this revelation has made me understand that none of my past failures mean anything to him, as he loves me loves so more than anything I could ever do for him. The relationship that he so desires to have with us must come first above all things in life, whether that's the things in life that we are doing for him or any other relationship that he has allowed us to have. Seeking a relationship with God is the first and foremost thing we should be pursuing, and everything else in life will just fall into order after that.

I'm not saying that I expect the rest of my life to not be filled with any more valleys, but I do expect that my walk with the Lord will be a closer one than I had before; thank you, Jesus. As I reflect back on all the experiences that I've had in life and how God has truly been there every step of the way, I can see how he has been guiding and protecting me. I have a deeper sense of how much he truly does love me and that the relationship that he wants to have with me is so much more personal than what I have allowed in the past. The fire that I have deep inside of me now is one that is filled with a desire to be closer to God, a desire to know him in a more intimate way. As I'm seeking a closer walk with Jesus, the Holy Spirit is developing the friendship that God so desires to have with me.

The love that he has for us when he opens up certain doors is born out of the same love he has when he closes others. He is such a loving God and always knows what's best for us at every stage of our lives, and he's always prompting us to take the path that we should. Even when we make wrong decisions, he never stops caring about us, no matter how hard we struggle with what he has laid before us. The cares of this world are falling off my heart just like the scales that fell off of Apostil Paul's eyes when he was allowed to see again.

These are the days in which God is calling his children to rise up and take their rightful places in the kingdom of heaven. The Holy Spirit is moving about from place to place, causing a revival in the hearts and minds of his believers all across the world like never before. First and foremost, he wants us to call out to him and be satisfied with who he is and what he has done for us, not who we are or what we can do for him. He wants us to focus on how much he loves us, not how much we love him. In doing so, we will be filled with the unspeakable joy that is the strength of our salvation, the joy that can only come from such a loving God.

As I enter the next season of my life, I'm filled with a spirit of anticipation that God is working everything out for his purpose, pouring out his spirit upon his children as he calls us to a deeper understanding of who he is. When we come to a greater understanding of the love he has for us, we are able to see just how free he has truly made us.

"So if the Son sets you free, you will be free indeed."

John 8:36

www.ingramcontent.com/pod-product-compliance
Lightning Source LLC
Chambersburg PA
CBHW041318110526
44591CB00021B/2827